Evaluation of anti-microbial and anti-oxidant and phytochemical activity of *Eupatorium triplinerve* Vahl *against wound infections*

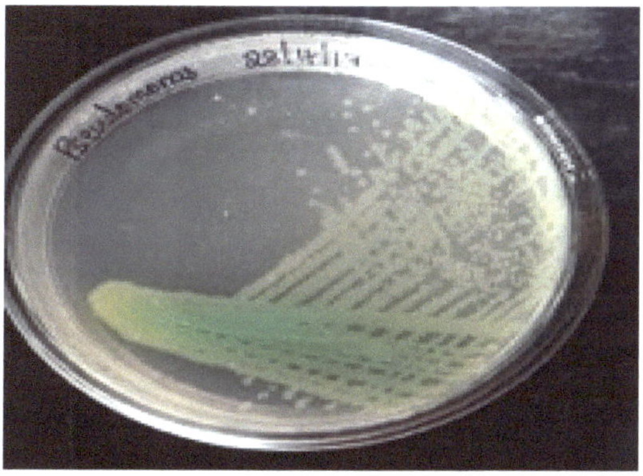

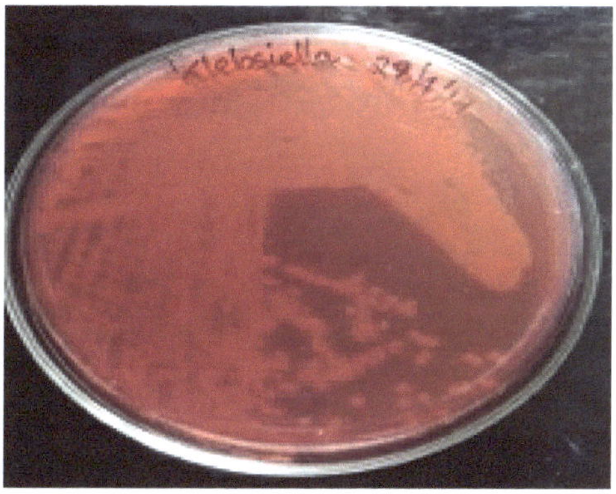

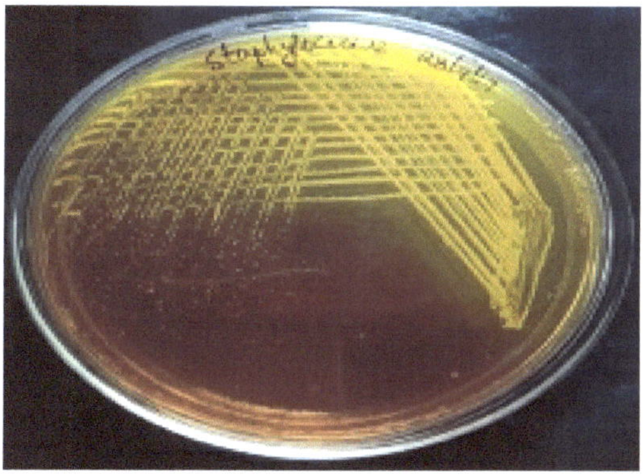

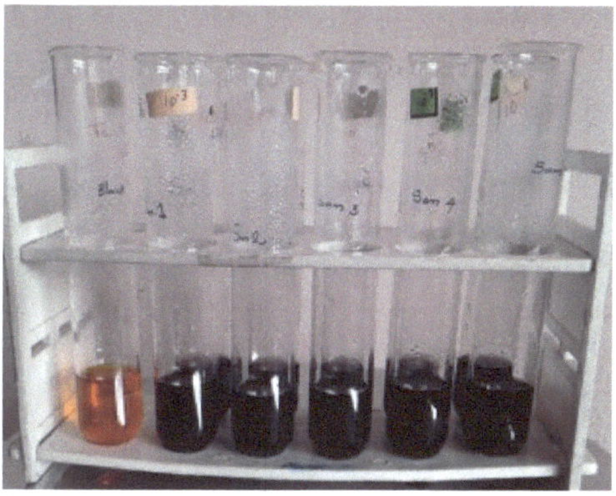

Prem Jose Vazhacharickal, John Joseph and Athira Vasanthan

Table of contents

Table of figures

Table of tables

List of abbreviations

°C	: Degree Celsius
BA	: Blood Agar
$FeCl_3$	: Ferric Chloride
H_2SO_4	: Sulphuric acid
HCl	: Hydrochloric acid
LF	: Lactose Fermentation
MA	: Mac-Conkey Agar
mg	: Milligram
MHA	: Muller Hinton Agar
Mm	: Millimeter
MR	: Methyl Red
NA	: Nutrient Agar
$NaHCO_3$	: Sodium bicarbonate
NaOH	: Sodium hydroxide
PSM	: Plants Secondary Metabolites
TLC	: Thin layer chromatography
TSI	: Triple Sugar Iron
UV	: Ultra Violet
VP	: Voges Proskauer
WHO	: World Health Organization
µg	: Microgram

Evaluation of anti-microbial, anti-oxidant and phytochemical activity of *Eupatorium triplinerve* Vahl against wound infections

Prem Jose Vazhacharickal[1]*, John Joseph[2] and Athira Vasanthan[2]
* premjosev@gmail.com
[1]Department of Biotechnology, Mar Augusthinose College, Ramapuram, Kerala, India-686576

[2]Department of Bioscience, Indira Gandhi College of Arts and Science, Nellikuzhi, Kerala, India-686691

Abstract

Medicinal plants have bioactive compounds which are used for various human disease and also an important role in wound healing. The present study is to investigate about the Antimicrobial, phytochemical and antioxidant activity of *Eupatorium triplinerve* Vahl. The extracts are studied against human wound and burn pathogenic bacterial stains. *E. coli*, *Klebsiella species*, *Pseudomonas species*, *Staphylococcus aureus*, *Enterobacter species*. From the phytochemical study is shows the presence of steroids, glycosides, tannins, phenols, saponins and flavonoids. Plant extracts compounds were separated by thin layer chromatography and identification based on Rf values. The presence of vitamin C play and important role of antioxidants.

Keywords: *Eupatorium triplinerve* Vahl, Rf values, Thin Layer Chromatography, Antimicrobial activity.

1. Introduction

Ayurveda is commonly known as the science of longevity and it is oldest and available Method of treatment in India. Ayu means life, veda means knowledge. Ayurveda is a combination of the soul, mind and the body. Ayurveda concepts appeared and developed between 2500 and 500 BC in India. The literal meaning of Ayurveda is "Science of life" because ancient Indian system of health care focused views of man and his illness. It is pointed out that the positive health means metabolically well balanced human beings. according to Ayurveda, the discare evolves from the body due to external factors. It has a vast literature is Sanskrit covering all aspects of discuses, pharmacy and therapeutics. Its main aim is the preservation for normal persons and treatment of sick individuals using only natural Methods.

Charka, Sahrutha, Vagbhata, Madhava and sharangadhara were the great Acharya or scholars of Ayurvedic medicines. They had great power of observation, generalization and analysis. The principles of Ayurvedic treatment are same as that of Allophathic treatment. They consist of removing the injurious agent, smoothing injured body and mind eradicating the cause. The difference lies in the methods of detail adopted by the different Systems. In Ayurveda great importance is given upon the study of various stages of vitiation of the Doshas. The three doshas are – Vatha (wind) Pittu (bile) and Kapha (phlegm). The seven Dhatus are –Rasa (Chyle), Raktha (blood), mamsa (Flesh), Medas (fat), Asthi (bone), Majja (marrow) and sukla (sperm). The three malas are sweat, urine and excreta. Disease according to Ayurveda is generally defined as disarrangement of the three Doshas. Health is an equilibrium of the three Doshas. Ayurveda shows the way to remove diseases to keep up health and attain longevity.

Medicinal plants which from the back bone of traditional medicine have in the last few decades been the subject of very intense pharmacological studies. This has been brought about by the acknowledgement of the value of medicinal plant as potential source of new compounds of therapeutic value and as a source of new compounds in drug development. In many parts of the world medicinal plants are used for antibacterial, antifungal, antiviral activities.

Medicinal plant are still parts of traditional medicinal systems in developing in countries many infections disease are known to be treated with herbal remedied throughout the history of mankind. Even today plant materials continue to play a major role in primary health plants infection disease is the number one among all cause of death, according approximately one day deaths throughout the world. About 50-75 % of hospital deaths are reported due to infections disease. There numbers are still increasing due to developments of resistance in microorganisms to the existing first line drug (Akinpelu et al., 2008).

1.1 *Eupatorium triplinerve* Vahl (Ayapana)

Ayapana is an evergreen perennial plant that has its origin from south America. It also grows in Brazil, Peru, Ecuador, Puerto Rico, Hawaii and India. It is a common ornamental plant with great medicine value. But apart from the fancy valve that it holds, it has many medicinal benefits also. Ayapana is the common Ayurvedic name *Eupatorium triplinerve*, belongs to Asteraceae family.

It is a tropical American shrub that is commonly known as water hemp. The plant bears long and slender leaves which are used to make herbal medicinal extract. The stem is hairless and reddish colour. The leaves are purple, occur in corymbose inflorescence and glabrous. Ayappana is known as vishalya karni in English. It is used to control bleeding from open wounds clothing. The leaves and stem are indicated in bloody diarrhoea, bleeding piles, stomach ulcer, bleeding or any other part of the body. The leaves contain volatile oil, ayapana oil etc . The plant yields many chemicals such as coumarian chemicals, cincol, alpha hilandrena, alpha terncol, ayapanin, ayapin, borneol, coumarin, sabinene, umbelliferone and many other. Hemarin, an important bio-chemical extract of this plant is used to make anti-tumour medications. The leaves of Ayapana contain many essential oils, coumarins, ayapanins and ayapin. Additionally vitamin C and Carotene are also found in this plant.

1.2 Taxonomical classification (*Eupatorium triplinerve* Vahl; Ayappana)

Kingdom: Plantae-- planta, plantes, plants, vegetal

Subkingdom: Viridiplantae

Superdivision: Embryophyta

Division: Tracheophyta

Class: Magnoliopsida

Order: Asterales

Family: Asterceae

Genus: Ayapana

Species: *Eupatorium triplinerve* Vahl

1.3 Special activity

- Ayapana has a general detoxifying effect on the body. It helps revive liver function and cleanse all body . This way it helps to rejuvenate the cells and tissues of the body . Increasing the longevity and vitality of the body.
- Ayapana has antiseptic properties which help in healing wounds an preventing formation of ulcerations.
- When consumed orally it helps prevent bleeding any part of the body. It also helps heal ulceration anywhere inside the gut , preventing bleeding it can therefore be very helpful in discases like gastric and two duodenal ulcer, crohns descase , IBS haemarrhoids , anal fistula etc.
- Ayapana is great for clearing out the bowels , it helps prevent colite and inflammation in the intestines due to its pilta shamak properties when the intestines are clear and healthy, skin condition improves and abdominal problems like acidity, gastritis and bloating can be easily relieved. Even in cases of large abdominal distension such as ascites , it can be given to the patient.
- Ayapana leaves have properties that can manage fever cough and cold naturally.
- whole parts of the plant including the stem ,leaves and roots can be made in to a decoction to relieve malarial fever.
- For insect bites ,wounds and bleeding both internal or external or ,sterile paste of Ayapana leaves can be very handy.

- Oral health problems like gingivitis and stomatitis can be relieved with the use of fresh juice of the leaves of this plant.
- Ayapana is a great option for managing menstrual irregularities in females . And helps regulate the hormonal in balance and strengthens the female reproductive system.
- Laboratory studies conducted on the leaf extracts of this plant have shown a considerable degree of antifungal and anti-microbial effects.

1.4 Word of caution

Ayapana should be avoided by people taking blood thinner. The leaves contain a highly aromatic chemical known as coumarin which has blood thinning and anti-coagulant properties. People on blood thinner can develop an increased risk of bleeding or stroke in such a care.

1.5 Phytochemicals

According to the world health organization, a medicinal plant is any plant which, in one or more of its organs ,contains substance that can be used for therapeutic purposes ,or which are precursors for chemo – pharmaceutical semi synthesis. Such a plant will have its parts including leaves, roots, rhizomes, stems, barks, flowers, fruits, grains or seeds, employed in the control of treatment of disease condition and there for contains chemical components that are medically active. These non-nutrients plant chemical compounds or bioactive compound are often referred to as phyto chemicals or phyto constituents and are responsible for protecting the plant against microbial infections.

Plant are natural reservoir of medicinal agents almost free from the side effect normally caused by synthetic chemicals. The world health organization estimates that herbal medicine is still the main stay of about 75-80% of the world population mainly in the developing countries from primary health care because of better cultural acceptability better compatibility with the human be and lesser side effects (Kimbiji, 2000) The over use of synthetic drugs with impurities resulting in linger incidence of adverse drug reaction has motivated mankind to go back to nature for safer remedies. Due to varied locations where these plants grow , coupled with the problems of different vernacular names, the world health organization published standards for herbal safety to minimize adulteration and a base .

1.6 Antimicrobial activity

Antimicrobial activity was carried out using Agar well diffusion method. methanol and distilled water were used as solvents for the extraction of the Muller Hinton Agar (MHA) media is considered to the best for routine susceptibility testing of non-fastidious bacteria for the many reason. About 20 ml of MHA medium poured in the sterilized petridishes and allowed to solidity. The agar medium was spread with 24 hours cultured microbial strains by sterilized swabs well of approximately 6mm were made in the culture medium using sterile well puncture. 50ml of the plant extracts was added to the wells, gentamycin disc as control for the cultures. The plates were incubated aerobically for 24 hours. Sensitivity of the organisms to the extract was recorded.

1.7 Anti-oxidant activity

Antioxidants are the substance, that inhibits oxidation especially to counteract deterioration of stored food products, otherwise a substance such as vitamin C or E that removes potentially damaging oxidizing agent in a living organism.

1.8 Thin layer chromatography (TLC)

Thin layer chromatography (TLC) is a simple quick and inexpensive procedure that gives the chemist a quick answer as to how many components are in a mixture. TLC is also used to support the identity of a components in a mixture when the Rf a compound is compared with the Rf of a known compound (Preferably both run on the plate is a steel of glass metal or plastic which is coated with a thin layer of a solid adsorbent (silica or alumina) A small amount of the mixture to be analysed is spotted near the bottom of this plate. The TLC plate is them placed in a shallow pool of a solvent in a developing chamber so that only the very bottom of plate is in the liquid. This liquid , or the solvent is the mobile phase, and slowly rises up the TLC plate by capillary action.

As the solvent moves past the spot that was applied, an equilibrium is established for each component of the mixture between the molecules of that component which are adsorbed on the solid and the molecules which are in solution. In principle the component will differ in solubility and in the strength of their adsorption to the adsorbent and some component will be carried further up the   plate of them others. When the solvent has reached the top of the plate, the plate is removed from the developing chambers dried and the separated component are colured visualizations is straight forward. Usually the compounds are not colored, so a UV lamp is utilised to visualize the plates (the plate contains a fluorescent dye which glows everywhere except where an organic compound is on the plate).

1.9 Aim

To study the antimicrobial, antioxidant and phytochemical activity of *Eupatorium triplinerve vahl* extracts against wound infection.

1.10 Objectives

The objectives of the current research work are to characterize and evaluate the phytochemical and antimicrobial activity of *Eupatorium triplinerve* Vahl extract against wound infection.

2. Review of literature

Traditionally used medicinal plants have recently attracted the attention of the Pharmaceutical and scientific communities. This has involved the isolation and identification of secondary metabolites produced by pants and their use as active principles in medical preparation. Many of the plants secondary metabolites are consecutive existing in healthy plants in their biologically active. Forms but other occur as inactive precursors and are active in response to tissue damage or pathogen attack. The array of secondary metabolites produced by plants is daunting with wide ranging chemical, physical and biological activities. These consecutive a source of bioactive substances and presently scientific interest has increased dues to the search for new drugs of plants origin. A number of Plants Secondary Metabolites (PSM) have been used as anticancer agents. Flavonoid-rich extracts from the mature roots of *Scutellaria biacalensis* have been shown exhibit anti-proliferative effect on various cancers lines. Taxol, a diterpene form the pacific yew has been widely used as drug for the treatment of ovarian and breast cancer. Limonoids, a group of triterpenes, have been shown to be successful in treatments with in vitro bioassays on human tumour cell lines, with limonin and isofraxinellone being the most active compounds. A lot of investigation has been conducted for natural antimicrobial agents. According to the World Health Organization (WHO) medical plants.

The indigenous system of medicine namely ayurvedic, siddha and unani has been existence for several centuries. This system medicine supports the need of more than 70% of population residing in the rural areas. Besides the demands made by these systems as there raw materials the demands of medicinal plants made by the modern pharmaceutical industries have also increased manifold since a long period of time, plants have been a valuable source of natural products for maintaining human health and infections control because, microbial infections pose a health problem throughout the world, and plants are a possible source of antimicrobial agents. Many of the herbs and spices used by humans to season food yield useful medicinal compounds. Microbial infections pose a health problem throughout the world, and plants are a possible source of antimicrobial agents.

Medicinal plants contain active principles which can be used as an alternative to cheap and effective herbal drugs against common bacterial infections mainstream medicine is increasingly receptive to the use of antimicrobial and other drugs derived plants, as traditional and antibiotics become ineffective and as new, particularly viral diseases remain intractable to this type of drug. Another driving factor for the renewed interest in plant antimicrobials in the past 20 years has been the rapid rate of species extinction. There is a feeling among natural products chemists and microbiologists alike that the multitude of potentially useful phytochemical structures which could be synthesized chemically is at risk of being lost irretrievably.

The intensive use of natural as primary health remedies due to their pharmacological properties are quite common. Natural products are preferred for biologically many infection disease are known to have been treated with herbal remedies through the history of mankind. The investigation in to the efficiency of plants based drugs has been paid attention because of their few side effects; cheap and easy availability. The plants used in traditional medicine areas still a large source of natural antioxidant, antimicrobial, anticancer agents that might serve as leads for the development of novel drugs. Natural crude drugs extracts and biological active compound isolated from plates species used in traditional can be prolific resources for such new drugs. Microorganism have been development resistant to many antibiotics due to the indiscriminate used of antimicrobial drugs inducing thus increase in problems with clinical treatment of infection used disease. In addition antibiotic area sometimes associated with adverse effects of the host who includes hypersensitivity.

Depletion of gut and mucosal microorganism, immunosuppressant and allergic reaction. There for there is a need for alternative antimicrobial drugs for the treatment of infection disease. One approach is to screen local medicinal plants for possible antimicrobial properties. Medicinal herbs represent source from which novel antibacterial and antifungal chemotherapeutic agents may be obtained. Due to alarming increase in the rate of infection with antibiotics resistant the microorganism and due to side effects of some synthetic antibiotics there is an increasing interest in medicinal plant accumulate to synthetic.

Many higher plants accumulate extractable organic substance in quantities sufficient to be economically useful as pharmaceuticals. species of ayappana higher plants were less much surveyed for antibacterial activity. *Eupatorium triplinerve* Vahl or *Eupatorium ayappana* familiarly known as ayyappana in Malayalam language belongs to the family. Asterance and is an ornamental plant. The essential coast of the plant has been reported to possess a number of medical properties such as nervous system, (CNS) depressed analgesic and sedative effects (Kokate et al., 1971). The metanolic extract of *E. trplinerve* showed hepato protective effect and antioxidant effect against carbon tetracholoride induced hepatotoxicity in rats (Bose et al., 2007) the ethanolic extract of the entire plant was active against *Bacillus subtilis* (Verpoorte et al., 1987). Marginal antimicrobial effect of petroleum – ether extract against various strains of bacteria and fungi were noted (Gupta et al., 2002). An ethanolic extract and its fractions from *Eupatorium triplinerve* have been reported to exhibit analgesic effect in inflammatory model of pain (Cheriyan et al., 2009).

Phytochemical are non-nutritive plant chemicals that contains certain protective, disease preventing compounds. More than 900 different photochemical have been identified as compounds of food, and many more phytochemical continue to be discovered today. Researchers have long known plants that there are physiochemical present for protection in plants but it has only been recently that they are being recommended for protection against human disease.

It is expected that plant extracts showing target sites other than those used by antibiotics will be active against drug resistant microbial pathogens. However, very little information is available on such activity of medicinal plants and out of the 4,00,000 plant spices on earth, only a small number has been systematically investigated for their antimicrobial activities.

Most of the synthetic drugs cause side effects and also most of the microbes developed resistant against the synthetic drugs, To alleviate this problems, antimicrobial compounds from potential plants should be explored. These drugs form plants are less toxic, side effects are scanty and also cost effective. They are effective in the treatment infectious disease. Hence, in this study, same efforts are continued in the progression of searching novel therapeutics.

In indigenous system of medicine the leaves of *Eupatorium triplinerve* are reported to be useful in pain and inflammatory disorders. However it traditional claims have not been fully validated. Hence the present study was designed evaluate the potential analogical and anti-inflammatory activity of *Eupatorium triplinerve*.

3. Hypothesis

The current research work is based on the following hypothesis

1) The extracts of *Eupatorium triplinerve* Vahl possess good antimicrobial and anti-oxidant properties.
2) The extracts could be used for the treatment of wound infections.

4. Materials and Methods

4.1 Study area

Kerala state covers an area of 38,863 km^2 with a population density of 859 per km^2 and spread across 14 districts. The climate is characterized by tropical wet and dry with average annual rainfall amounts to 2,817 ± 406 mm and mean annual temperature is 26.8°C (averages from 1871-2005; Krishnakumar et al., 2009). Maximum rainfall occurs from June to September mainly due to South West Monsoon and temperatures are highest in May and November.

4.2 Collection of samples

The sample *Eupatorium triplinerve* plant were collected from local areas of Idukki District, Kerala, India. The plants in grow bags and the leaves are collected from local areas. The leaves were cleaned thoroughly and dried at sunshade for 4-5 days. The dried samples were powdered using an electrical grinder. The powered samples were stored in screw caped bottles.

4.3 Preparation of methanolic and aqueous extracts
4.3.1 Methanol extraction

25 gm of powdered sample was taken in a soxhelt apparatus. The extraction process was carried out for two hours. Volume of the solution was taken in to the glass beaker. This methanol extract separated by methanol and extract using distillation process.

4.3.2 Aqueous extraction

150 ml soxhlet extractor is filled with approximately 25 g of dried leaf powder. Distilled water was used as a solvent for the extraction. The Extraction was carried out for two hours. Volume of the solution was reduced to heating, the excess water removed from the extract.

4.4 Clinical sample collection

Wound samples were collected from nearby clinical laboratory. The samples were transported immediately to the laboratory for further study.

4.5 Isolation of microorganisms

Wound samples were collected for the isolation of suspected organism, the samples were directly inoculated in to Nutrient agar, Mac-conkey agar and Blood agar plates. Incubate the plates at 37°C for 24 hours. After incubation colonies were selected to study their morphological characters and identification procedures are carried out.

4.6 Identification of pathogen
4.6.1 Colony characteristics

After incubation colony characteristics of the typical isolated colonies were studied. Colony characteristics such as size, forms, margin and opacity, consistency, pigmentation, lactose fermentation and haemolysis were studied.

4.6.2 Gram staining

1. Smear of the isolates are prepared in clean slide.
2. It is air dried and heat fixed.
3. The smear is flooded with crystal violet for 1 minute and then washed away with water.
4. Then smear is flooded with Grams iodine for 1 minute.
5. Then it is washed ways with decolourising agent such as 95% alcohol or acetone and washed with water.
6. Flood the smear with counter stain safranin and keep for 45 seconds and then washed with water.
7. The smear is air dried and observe under oil immersion objective.

4.6.3 Motility

1. Apply vaseline or paraffin wax at the edge of the cover slip.

2.Using a clean loop aseptically transfer a loop full of culture on cover slip.

3.Invert the cavity slide over the cover slip and press down to make firm seal.

4. Quickly and carefully turn down the slide so that drop is suspended in to cavity.

5.Examine drop by first locating edge of drop by focus it under the low power objective.

6. Reduce the light to see the edges as bright waxy line. against grey background. Then to high power and focus the edges of the drop to see motile and non- motile bacteria at the edge of the drop.

4.7 Biochemical characteristics
4.7.1 Sugar fermentation

    i)   Prepare sugar solution (sterile 1% sugar in 2% peptone water base with bromocresol purple indicator and inverted durhams tube.

    ii) Use a sterile pasteur pipette to inoculate the medium.

    iii) Alternatively the medium can be inoculated with a charged wire loop.

    iv) After inoculation, tubes were incubated overnight.

4.7.2 indole production-Kovac's method

    i.   Peptone broth was inoculated with the best organism.

    ii. Incubate at 37°C for 24 hours.

    iii. Add 0.5 ml kovacs reagent through the slides of the test tube.

4.7.3 Methyl red test

    i)   Inoculate the MR-VP medium with the test organism.

    ii) Incubate at 35°C for 24 hours.

    iii) After incubation, add 3 drops of methyl red indicator and mix well.

4.7.4 Triple sugar iron agar test

    i.   The TSI agar slant is inoculated by means of stab and streak method.

    ii. Inoculate the isolates in the butt by using a straight needle.

    iii. The slant surface is then streaked following incubation determines the fermentative activities of the organism.

4.7.5 Mannitol motility medium test

    i.   The medium is inoculated by stabbing the center of the tubes to its base.

    ii. Incubate at 35 + 2°C for 18-24 hours.

4.7.6 Urease test

    i.   Inoculate urea agar with the test organism.

    ii.   incubate at 37°C for 24 hours.

4.7.8 Nitrate reduction test

    i)   Streak the nutrient agar slant with test organism.

    ii)   Incubate 37°C at 24 hours.

    iii)   Mix equal volume of regent 1 and 11 in a test tube immediately before use.

    iv)   Add 3 or 4 drops of the mixture to the culture.

4.7.9 Catalase test

    i)   Place one drop of H_2O_2 on a clean glass slide.

    ii)   pick one colony from the solid media the help of sterile applicator stick.

    iii)   place the colony in H_2O_2 taken on a slide.

4.7.10 Oxidase test

    i)   Place the strip of filter paper on clean petridish.

    ii)   Add2-3dropoffreshlypreparedoxidase reagent

    iii)   The colony to be tested was picked with applicator stick and smeared over the oxidase paper.

4.7.11 Coagulase test

    i.   place a drop of physiological saline on both ends of the slide

    ii.   Emulsified a colony of the test organism in each of the drops to make thin suspension.

    iii.   Add a drop of plasma to one of the suspension and mix gently

    iv.   check for clumping of organism with in 1 minute.

4.8 Phytochemical analysis of *Eupatorium triplinative Vahl*

Phytochemical screening was done in order to detect the presence of bioactive constituents such as steroids, glycosides, tannins, phenols, saponins, flavonoids etc. using the methods described by Sofowora (1978) Trease and Evans (1989).

4.8.1 Test for steroids (Salkowaski test)

Salkowaski reaction: To 2ml of aqueous solution of a plant extracts were taken, 1 ml of conc H_2SO_4 is added carefully along the side of the tube. A red colour produced in the aqueous layer will indicate the presence of steroid (rese and Evans 1989)

4.8.2 Test for glycoside

A small amount of aqueous solution of a plant extract is dissolved in 1 ml of water the aqueous NaOH solution is added . formation of yellow colour indicates the presence of glycoside (Trease and Evans 1989)

4.8.3 Test for Tannin (Ferric chloride test)

To 2 ml of aqueous solution of plant extracts a drop 5% aqueous solution of $FeCl_3$ are added. A bluish black colour, which disappears on addition a few ml of dilute H_2SO_4, is followed by the formation of yellow brown precipitate (Trease and Evans 1989).

4.8.4 Test for phenol

To 1 ml of aqueous solution of plant extract, 2 ml distilled water followed by a few drop of 10% aqueous solution of $FeCl_3$ is added . formation of blue colour or green colour indicates the presence of phenol.

4.8.5 Test for saponins

About 5 ml of each sample of extract is taken in a test tubes a drop of $NaHCO_3$ is added. the mixture is shaken vigorously and kept for 3 minutes, a honey comb like forth is formed and it shows the presence of saponins.

4.8.6 Test for flavonoids

To In a test tube containing 0.5ml of each sample of extract is taken in test tube add 5-10 drops of diluted HCl and a small piece of zinc or magnesium are added the solution is boiled for a few minutes. Formation of red colour indicates the presence of flavonoid.

4.9 Antimicrobial screening
4.9.1 Agar well diffusion method

The agar well diffusion method of antibiotic sensitivity test in the most practical method for testing the antimicrobial activity of plant extract.

4.9.2 Antimicrobial activity

The antimicrobial assay was carried out using agar well diffusion method. Gentamycin is universal antibiotic disc used a drug, and corresponding solvents methanol and water are used as positive control. About 20 ml MHA medium for bacteria was poured in the sterilized petridishes and allowed to solidify. The agar medium was spread with 24 hours cultured microbial strains by sterilized swabs. well of 6mm in diameters were made in the culture medium using sterile well picture. About 50μl of the plant extracts (1mg/ml) was added to the wells. plates were the incubated at 37°C for 24 hours. Antimicrobial activity was evaluated by measuring the inhibition zone diameter in mm in to the well.

4.9.3 Preparation of oil

25 g of dry leaves mixed with 400 ml of distilled water, mixed and boiling for 2 hour. Then the mixture in filtered using filter paper. The filtrate is again mixed with distilled water and boiling in 2 hours . The filtrate is discarded, about 500 ml of extract mixed with 100ml coconut oil and boiling in a wide mouth container. To complete evaporation of water content. The oil extract is filter and preserved on a sterile bottle.

4.10 Thin layer chromatography

TLC is a simple, quick and inexpensive procedure that gives the chemist a quick answer to how many components are in a mixture. TLC is also used to support the identity of a compound in a mixture when the R1 of a compound is compared with Rf of a known compound.

4.10.1 Step 1: prepare the developing container

The developing container for TLC can be a specially designed chamber a jar with a lid or, a beaker with a watch glass on the top. pour solvent in to the in to the chamber to a depth of just less than 0.5 cm. To aid in the saturation of the TLC chamber with solvent vapours , line a part of the inside beaker with filter paper. Cover the beaker with a watch glass , swirl it gently , and allow it to stand while prepare the TLC plate.

4.10.2 Step 2: prepare the TLC plate

TLC plates used in the organic chemistry teaching labs. Each large sheet is cut horizontally in to plates, which are 5 cm tall by various widths. the more sample to run on plate. The wider it needs to be, handle the plates carefully so that do not disturber the coating of adsorbent or get them dirty. measure 0.5 cm from the bottom of the plate. Using a pencil, draw a line across the plate at the 0.5 cm mark. this is the origin. under the line, mark lightly the name of the samples spot on the plate.

4.10.3 Step 3: spot the TLC plate

If the sample is not already in solution dissolve about 1mg / 1ml of a volatile solvent such as hexanes, ethyl acetate, or methylene chloride. As a rule of thumb, a concentration of 1 % usually work well for TLC analysis. If the sample is too concentrated, it will run as a smear or streak obtained a microcapillary. This example plate has been spotted with 4 different quantities of the 2 extract and oils ready to develop.

4.10.4 Step 4: develop the TLC plate

Place the prepared TLC plate is the developing beaker, cover the beaker, cover the beaker with the watch glass and leaves it undistance on bench top. The solvent will rise up the TLC plate by capillary action. Allow the plate to develop until the solvent is about half a centimetre below the top of the plate. Remove the plate from the beaker and immediately mark solvent front with a pencil. Allow the plate to dry.

4.10.5 Step 5: visualise the spots on TLC plate

If there are any colored spots circle them pencil most samples are coloured and visualized with UV lamp. If the TLC plates runs samples which are too concentrated the spots will be streaked or run to get and measure the Rf values

Rf value = <u>Distance travelled by the compound</u>
Distance travelled by the solvent front

4.11 Antioxidant assay

Antioxidants are substances , that inhibits oxidation especially one used to counteract deterioration of stored food products, otherwise a substances such as vitamin C or E that removes potentially damaging oxidizing agent in living organism.

4.12 Vitamin C identification test

To 2ml of both methanol and aqueous extracts were taken, added 2ml of water 0.1 gm of sodium bicarbonate and 20mg of ferrous sulphate, shaken and allowed to stand. A deep violet colour is produced, added 5ml of 1m dilutedH_2SO_4 the colour disappeared.

4.13 Vitamin C assay

Weight accurately about 0.5ml extracts and dissolve in a mixture of 100ml of freshly boiled and cooled water and 25 ml of 1M H_2SO_4 immediately titrate with 0.05M iodine, using starch solution as indicator until a persistent blue- violet color is obtained.

4.14 Statistical analysis

The survey results were analysed and descriptive statistics were done using SPSS 12.0 (SPSS Inc., an IBM Company, Chicago, USA) and graphs were generated using Sigma Plot 7 (Systat Software Inc., Chicago, USA).

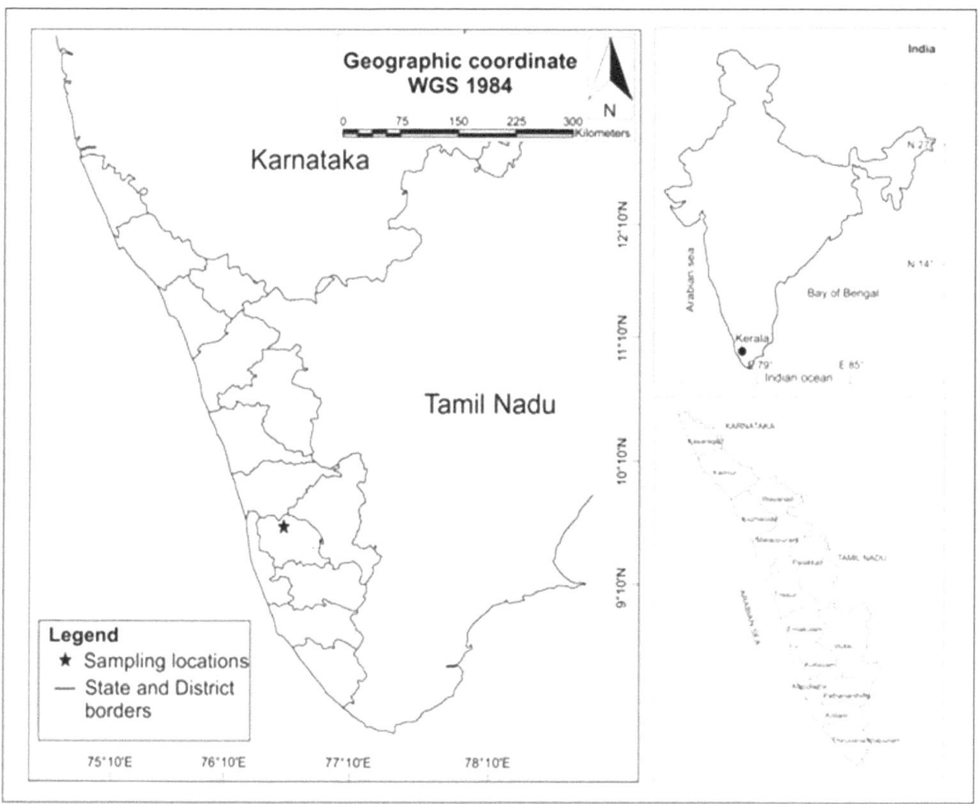

Figure 1. Map of Kerala showing the sample collection point. Authors own work.

Figure 2. Description of *Eupatorium triplinerve* Vahl a) plant in natural habitat, b) mature leaves, c) soxhlet extractor, d) distillation unit.

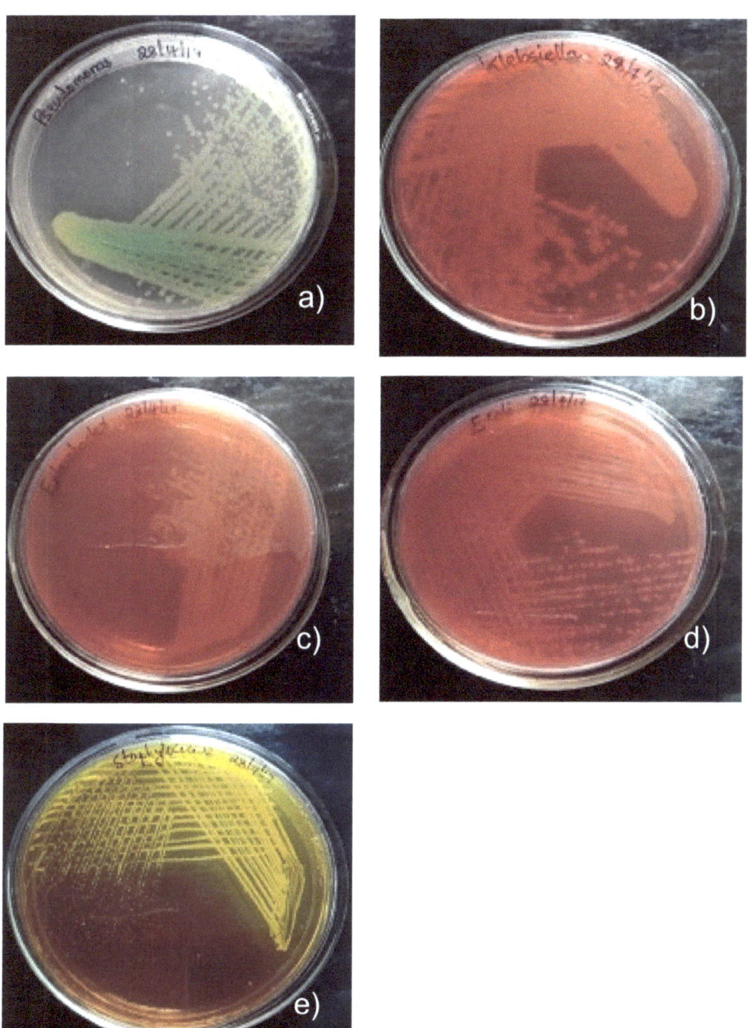

Figure 3. Isolated test organisms a) Pseudomonas species, b) Klebsiella species, c) Enterobacter species, d) *E. coli*, f) *Staphylococcus aureus*.

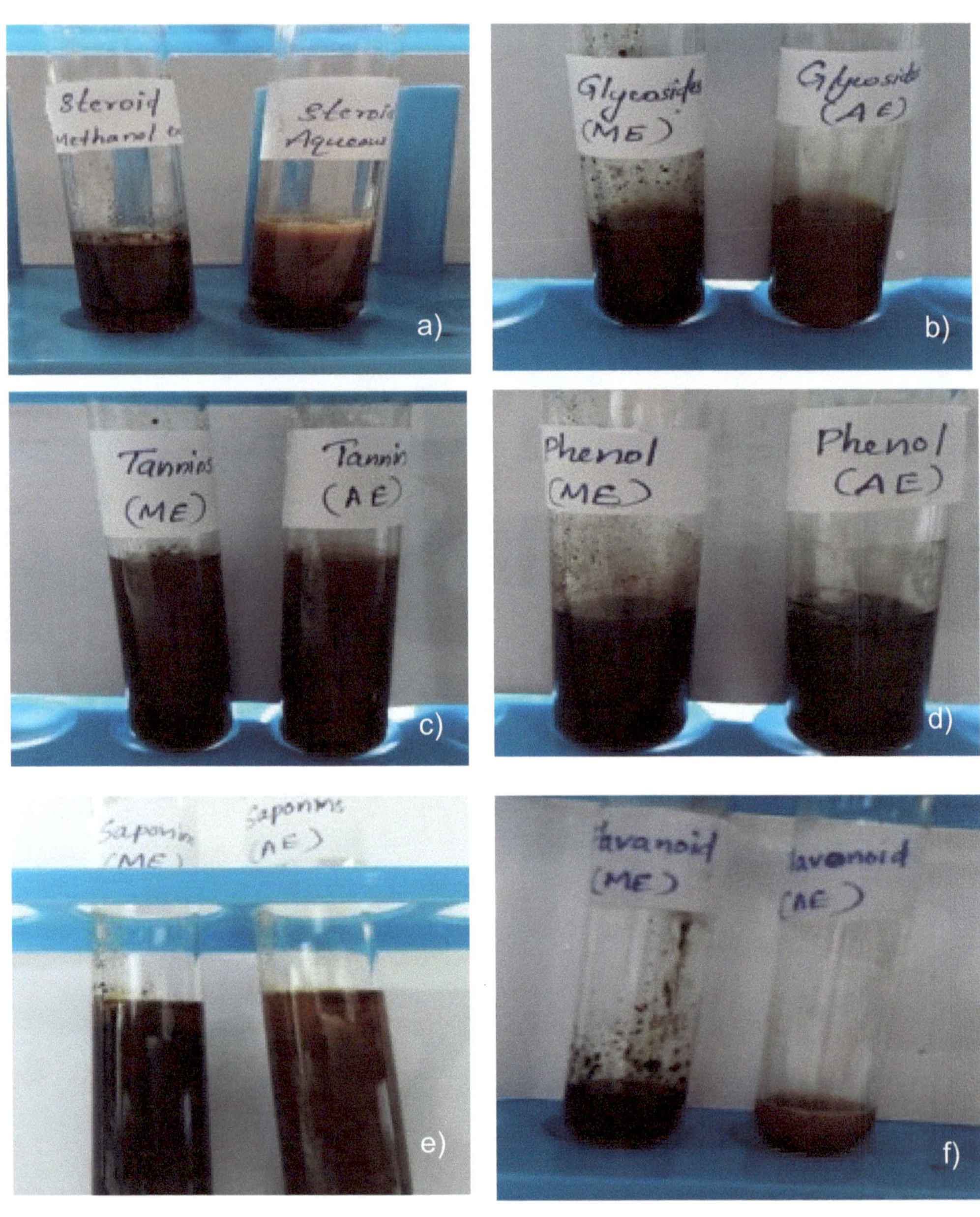

Figure 4. Description of phytochemical test using *Eupatorium triplinerve* Vahl extracts a) steroids, b) glycosides, c) tannins, d) phenols, e) saponins, f) flavonoids.

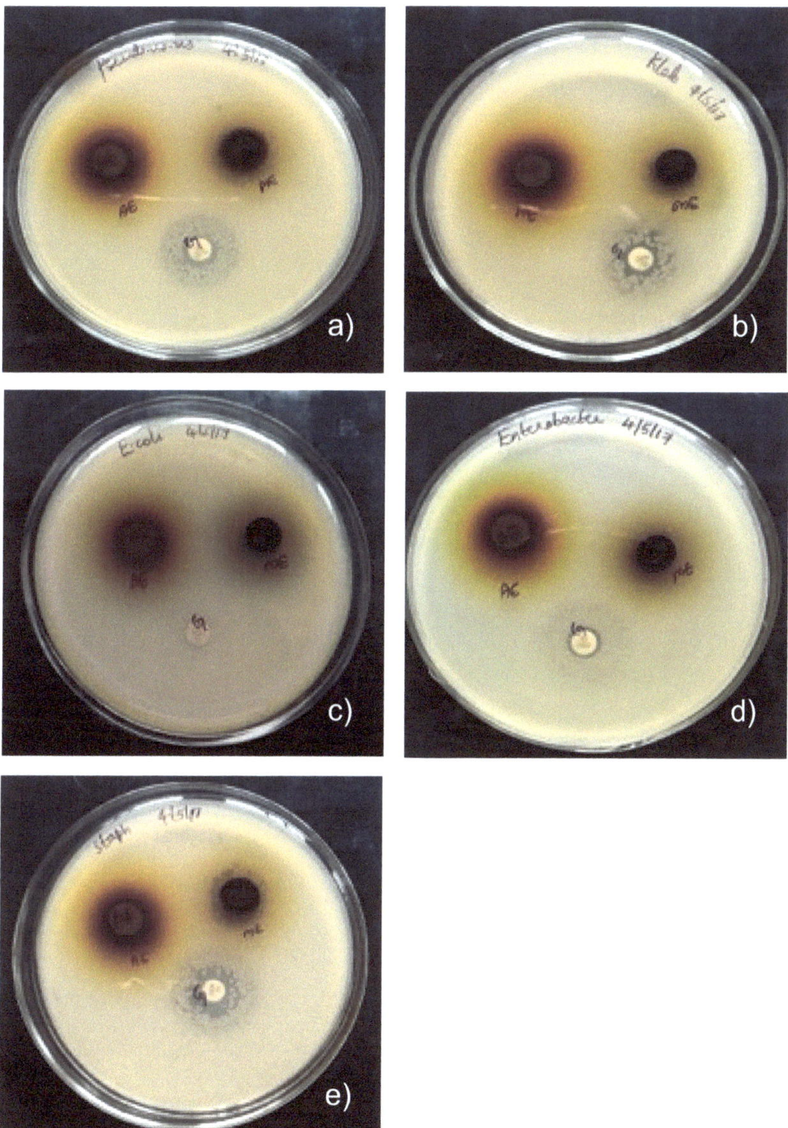

Figure 5. Antimicrobial activity of the Eupatorium triplinerve Vahl extract on Isolated test organisms a) Pseudomonas species, b) Klebsiella species, c) Enterobacter species, d) *E. coli*, f) *Staphylococcus aureus*.

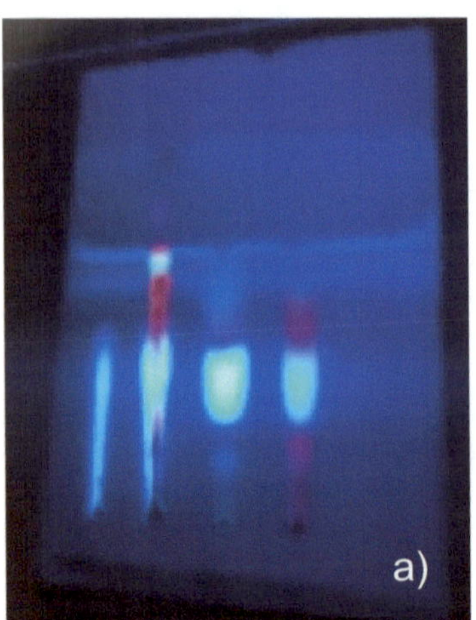
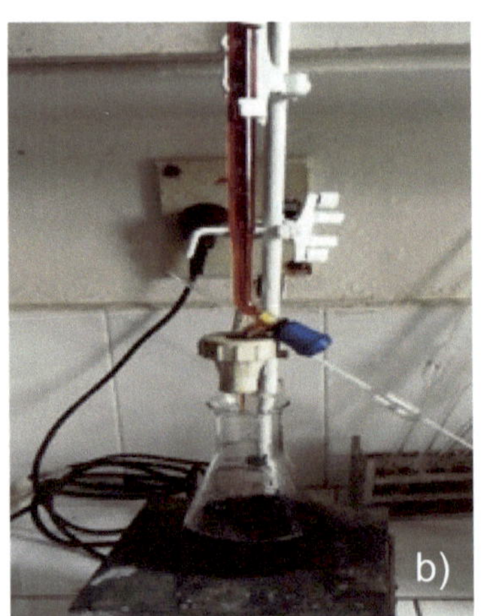

Figure 6. Description of *Eupatorium triplinerve* Vahl extract a) thin layer chromatography spots (lane 1: oil of aqueous extract; lane 2: aqueous extract; lane 3: oil of methanol extract; lane 4: methanol extract), b) antioxidant activity, c) identification tests.

Table 1. Colony morphology of the isolated organisms.

Sl No	Medium	Size	Shape	Margin	Elevation	Consistency	Opacity	LF	Haemolysis
Isolate 1	NA	small	circular	regular	Convex	Moist	Opaque	-	-
	MA	small	circular	regular	Convex	Moist	Opaque	Yes	-
	BA	small	circular	regular	Convex	Moist	Opaque	-	No
Isolate 2	NA	large	circular	Entire	Convex	Mucoid	Opaque	-	-
	MA	large	circular	Entire	Convex	Mocoid	Opaque	Yes	-
	BA	large	circular	Entire	Convex	Mucoid	Opaque	-	No
Isolate 3	NA	small	circular	regular	Convex	Moist	Translucent	-	-
	MA	small	circular	regular	Convex	Moist	Translucent	No	-
	BA	small	circular	regular	Flat	Moist	Translucent	-	Yes
Isolate 4	NA	small	circular	regular	Flat	Shiny	Opaque	-	-
	MA	small	circular	regular	Flat	Shiny	Opaque	Yes	-
	BA	small	circular	regular	Flat	Shiny	Opaque		beta haemolysis
Isolate 5	NA	large	circular	Entire	Convex	Mocoid	Opaque		
	MA	large	circular	Entire	Convex	Mucoid	Opaque	Yes	
	BA	large	circular	Entire	Convex	Mocoid	Opaque		

NA- Nutrient Agar; MA- Mac-Conkey Agar; BA- Blood Agar.; LF- Lactose Fermentation

Table 2. Direct microscopic examination of the isolated organisms.

SL No	Motility	Gram staining
Isolate 1	Motile rods	Gram negative rods
Isolate 2	Non motile rods	Gram negative rods
Isolate 3	Motile rods	Gram negative rods
Isolate 4	Non motile cocci	Gram positive cocci
Isolate 5	Motile rods	Gram negative rods

Table 3. Biochemical characterization of the isolated organisms.

Tests	Isolate 1	Isolate 2	Isolate 3	Isolate 4	Isolate 5
Glucose test	A/G	A/G	-	A/-	A/G
Lactose test	A/G	A/G	-	A/-	A/G
Sucrose test	A/G	A/G	-	A/-	A/G
Maltose test	A/G	A/G	-	A/-	A/G
Indole test	+	-	-	-	-
Methyl red test	+	-	-	+	-
Voges proskauer test	+	-	-	+	+
Citrate test	-	+	+	-	+
Triple sugar iron agar test	+/+G	+/+G	K/k	+/+	+/+G
Mannitol motility test	M/F	N/F	M/F	N/F	N/F
Urease test	-	+	+	+	+
Oxidase test	-	-	+	-	-
Catalase test	-	-	+	+	-
Coagulates test				+	

Isolate 1- *Escherichia coli*; Isolate 2- kKebsiella Species; Isolate 3- Pseudomonas species; Isolate 4-*Staphylococcus* aureus; Isolate 5- Enterobacter species

Table 4. Phytochemical screening of *Eupatorium triplinerve* Vahl extract.

Sl no	Chemical content	Methanol extract	Aqueous extract
1	Steroids	-	+
2	Glycosides	+	+
3	Tannins	+	+
4	Phenols	+	+
5	Saponins	+	+
6	Flavonoids	-	+

Table 5. Diameter of the zone of inhibition using antibiotic standards.

Organisms	Aqueous extract	Methanol extract	Gentamycin
Staphylococcus aureus	2.8 mm	2.1 mm	1.7 mm
Escherichia coli	2.7 mm	2.3 mm	0.8 mm
Klebsiella species	2.8 mm	2.0 mm	0.9 mm
Psuedomonas species	2.7 mm	2.2 mm	0.9 mm
Enterobacter species	2.7 mm	2.1 mm	0.8 mm

Table 6. Thin layer chromatography using toluene and ethyl acetate (9:1) and Rf values.

Sample	No of spots	Colour obtained	Rf values
Aqueous extract oil	2	Fluorescent green	0.21
		Fluorescent blue	0.35
Aqueous extract	8	Brown	0.14
		Brown	0.28
		Orange	0.46
		Fluorescent blue	0.51
		Red	0.59
		Red	0.64
		Fluorescent green	0.67
		Reddish orange	0.71
Methanol extract oil	3	Blue	0.25
		Fluorescent blue	0.42
		Yellowish orange	0.5
Methanol extract	4	Orange	0.15
		Orange	0.25
		Fluorescent blue	0.42
		Red	0.5

Toluene : Ethyl acetate   9:1

Table 7. Vitamin c (ascorbic acid) values obtained during antioxidant assay.

Extract	Concentration of Ascorbic acid (mg)
Aqueous extract	0.56
Methanol extract	0.34

5. Results

Eupatorium triplinerve Vahl extract were prepared in methanol and distilled water by soxhlet extraction method.

5.1 Isolation of bacterial pathogen

Isolation of bacterial pathogen from clinical wound samples. Total of 5 bacterial species was isolated from clinical wound samples. All the bacterial strains were identified based on their biochemical characteristics and colony morphology. The identified colonies were purified by quadrant streaking and corresponding medium.

5.2 Characterization of bacterial isolates

The wound samples where incubated aseptically in to Nutrient agar, Mac-Conkey agar and Blood agar media colonies were isolated.

5.3 Phytochemical analysis

The phytochemical study was revealed the presence of phytochemicals considered as active medicinal chemical constituents. The each sample contains the presence of steroids, glycosides, tannins, phenols, saponins and flavonoids.

5.4 Antimicrobial activity-Agar well diffusion method

The plant *Eupatorium triplinerve* Vahl were screened for potential antimicrobial activity against the pathogen. Methanol and aqueous extract showed more consistent antimicrobial activity. Generally most of the test organisms were sensitive to the methanol and aqueous extracts. Out of these extracts, aqueous extract shows more antibacterial activity against one or more bacteria. The inhibition of growth with the Gentamycin disc provided as control. Aqueous extract were most effective against *Staphylococcus aureus* and *Klebsiella species*.

5.5 Thin layer chromatography

The TLC studies of the extract and oils were considered. The extracts are more useful to find the presence of various chemical compounds of the plant. TLC study of extracts and oils show clear separation. The aqueous extract shows better Rf spots .

5.6 Antioxidant assay

Antioxidant assay of *Eupatorium triplinerve* Vahl extract were determined by titrimetric method. The extracts shows Ascorbic acid (Vitamin C) content.

5.7 Application of aqueous extract on wound and burn infection

Patient 1: Ajitha 23 years old had wound in her right hands. She applied with *Eupatorium triplinerve* Vahl aqueous extract directly. After 2 days the wound is healed.

Patient 2: Rajamma 53 years old female had burn in her arms, she applied with Eupatorium *triplinerve* Vahl aqueous extract, the 2-3 days the burn healed.

Patient 3: Mohanan 55 years old male had wound in his leg he applied with aqueous extract of *Eupatoirium triplinerve* Vahl; 3 days taken to recover.

Patient 4: Abhilash 30 years old male had wound in his left hand he applied with *Eupatorium triplinerve* Vahl aqueous extract few days the burn is healed.

6. Discussion

The methanol and aqueous extracts of *Eupatorium triplinerve* Vahl were taken for their antimicrobial, phytochemical, antioxidant activity studies.

The plant extract were screened for potential antimicrobial activity against wound infection. Methanol and aqueous extracts showed more consistent antimicrobial activity. Generally most of the test organisms were sensitive to the methanol and aqueous extracts.

The aqueous extract most effective against *Staphylococcus aureus* and *Klebsiella species*. The methanol extract most effective against *E.coli* and *Pseudomonas species*. The antibiotic disc Gentamycin most effective against *Staphylococcus aureus* and *E.coli*. The antimicrobial properties of medicinal plant are being increasingly reported from different parts of the world. The world health organization estimates that plant extract or their active constituents are used as medicine in traditional therapies of 80% of the world is population it is found that the activity is absent in the fraction as the dilution is reduced .

The phytochemical screening of *Eupatorium triplinerve* extracts showed the presence of steroids, glycosides, tannins, phenols, saponins and flavonoids. The bioactive secondary metabolites would have been responsible for the antimicrobial activity displayed by the *Eupatorium triplinerve* extracts. The aqueous extract shows more phytochemicals than methanol extract.

The antioxidant activity showing the presence of Ascorbic Acid (Vitamin C) in both extracts. Comparatively aqueous extract showing high content of Vitamin C, than methanol extract. This plant is a source of Vitamin C and has medicinal uses mainly anti- inflammatory, antibleeding, fever, reduce anti-diabetic and Disinfectant (Maurya and singh, 2010). The leaves stem, flower, roots of this plant used in herbal drugs, and show anti-helminthic, anti-tumour, antioxidant properties (Ayyanar and Ignacimuthu, 2008).

The thin layer chromatography studies of the extracts and oils were considered the extract are more useful to find the presence of various chemical compounds of the plant. TLC study of extracts and oils show clear separation, aqueous extract shows better Rf spots.

This study suggested that the less expensive, safe and effective natural extract of *Eupatorium triplinerve* Vahl are used against wound and burn infections.

7. Conclusions

The selected plant *Eupatorium triplinerve* Vahl contain potential antibacterial, phytochemical, antioxidant components that may be of great use for the development of pharmaceutical industries. The extract possess significant inhibitory effects against tested pathogens. The above results open the possibility of finding new clinically effective antioxidant drug and could be useful in understanding the relationship between the traditional cures and current medicines.

8. Future perspective

Further research is necessary to determine the identity of the antibacterial compounds from within these plant and also determine their efficiency. This study suggested that the less expensive, safe and effective natural extract used for this highly valuable medicinal plant to meet the increasing demand from traditional medicine system.

References

Sharma, A., Verma, R., & Ramteke, P. (2009). Antibacterial activity of some medicinal plants used by tribals against UTI causing pathogens. *World Applied Sciences Journal*, 7(3), 332-339.

Ayyanar, M., & Ignacimuthu, S. (2008). Medicinal uses and pharmacological actions of five commonly used Indian medicinal plants: A mini-review. *Iranian Journal of Pharmacology and Therapeutics*, 7(1), 107-0.

Barry, A. L. (1976). Principle & practice of Microbiology. Lea & Fabager, Philadelphia, 3, 21-25.

Bentley, G. A., Newton, S. H., & Starr, J. (1981). Evidence for an action of morphine and the enkephalins on sensory nerve endings in the mouse peritoneum. *British Journal of Pharmacology*, 73(2), 325-332.

Bauer, A. W., Kirby, W. M., Sherris, J. C., & Turck, M. (1966). Antibiotic susceptibility testing by a standardized single disk method. *American Journal of Clinical Pathology*, 45(4), 493.

Chanda, S., & Rakholiya, K. (2011). Combination therapy: Synergism between natural plant extracts and antibiotics against infectious diseases. Microbiol Book Series, 520-529.

Chatterjee, S. K., Bhattacharjee, I., & Chandra, G. (2011). Isolation and identification of bioactive antibacterial components in leaf extracts of *Vangueria spinosa* (Rubiaceae). *Asian Pacific Journal of Tropical Medicine*, 4(1), 35-40.

Cheriyan, B. V., Venkatadri, N., Viswanathan, S., & Kamalakannan, P. (2009). Screening of alcoholic extract of *Eupatorium triplinerve* Vahl and its fractions for its antinociceptive activity. *Indian Drugs*, 46(10), 797-802.

Selvamangai, G., & Bhaskar, A. (2012). GC–MS analysis of phytocomponents in the methanolic extract of *Eupatorium triplinerve*. *Asian Pacific Journal of Tropical Biomedicine*, 2(3), S1329-S1332.

Cheriyan, B. V., Venkatadri, N., Viswanathan, S., & Kamalakannan, P. (2009). Screening of alcoholic extract of *Eupatorium triplinerve* Vahl and its fractions for its antinociceptive activity. *Indian Drugs*, 46(10), 797-802.

Chorianopoulos, N., Kalpoutzakis, E., Aligiannis, N., Mitaku, S., Nychas, G. J., & Haroutounian, S. A. (2004). Essential oils of Satureja, Origanum, and Thymus species: chemical composition and antibacterial activities against foodborne pathogens. *Journal of Agricultural and Food Chemistry*, 52(26), 8261-8267.

Dahiya, P., & Purkayastha, S. (2011). Phytochemical screening and antimicrobial potentials of *Alangium salvifolium* and *Piper longum* against multidrug resistant bacteria from clinical isolates. *International Journal of Pharmacy and Pharmaceutical Sciences*, 3, 462-465.

Desai, M. N., & Chavan, N. S. (2010). Antibacterial activity and phytochemical screening of *Cynometra iripa* Kostel. International Journal of Pharmaceutical and Biological Sciences, 1(3), 1-4.

Dubuisson, D., & Dennis, S. G. (1977). The formalin test: a quantitative study of the analgesic effects of morphine, meperidine, and brain stem stimulation in rats and cats. *Pain*, 4(1), 161-174.

Ecobichon, D. J. (1997). The basis of toxicity testing. CRC press. New York, USA.

Seyyednejad, S. M., & Motamedi, H. (2010). A review on native medicinal plants in Khuzestan, Iran with antibacterial properties. *International Journal of Pharmacology*, 6(5), 551-560.

Fernie, A. R., Trethewey, R. N., Krotzky, A. J., & Willmitzer, L. (2004). Metabolite profiling: from diagnostics to systems biology. *Nature Reviews Molecular Cell Biology*, 5(9), 763.

Garg, S. C., & Nakhare, S. (1993). Studies on the essential oil from the flowers of *Eupatorium triplinerve*. Indian Perfumer, 37, 318-318.

Gupta, M., Mazumder, U. K., Chaudhuri, I., Chaudhuri, R. K., Bose, P., Bhattacharya, S., & Patra, S. (2002). Antimicrobial activity of Eupatorium ayapana. *Fitoterapia*, 73(2), 168-170.

Gupta R. Gabrielsen B, Ferguson! FM- Nature's Medicines: Traditional Knowledge and Intellectual Property Management_ Case Studies from the National Institutes of Health (NIH). USA Current Drug Discovery Technologies, 2, 2005, 203-219.

Munuswamy, H., Thirunavukkarasu, T., Rajamani, S., Elumalai, E. K., & Ernest, D. (2013). A review on antimicrobial efficacy of some traditional medicinal plants in Tamilnadu. *Journal of Acute Disease*, 2(2), 99-105.

Hunskaar, S., & Hole, K. (1987). The formalin test in mice: dissociation between inflammatory and non-inflammatory pain. *Pain*, 30(1), 103-114.

Khandelwal KR. (2000). Practical Pharmacognosy Techniques and Experiments, Nirali Prakashan, Pune, India.

Kokate, C. K., Rao, R. E., & Varma, K. C. (1971). Pharmacological studies on the essential oil of *Eupatorium triplinerve* Vahl. I. The effects on the central nervous system and antimicrobial activity. *Flavour Industry*, 2(3), 177-180.

Koster R, Anderson M and DeeBeer AJ. (1959). Acetic acid for analgesic screening. Fed Proc. 18: 412-416.

Kumara P.D, Jayewardene GL, Aluwiltare AP. (2001). Complete colonic duplication in an infant. Ceylon Med, J. 46:69-70.

Lee, S., Son, D., Ryu, J., Lee, Y. S., Jung, S. H., Kang, J., ... & Shin, K. H. (2004). Anti-oxidant activities ofacanthopanax senticosus stems and their lignan components. Archives of pharmacal research, 27(1), 106-110.

Mohana, D. C., Satish, S., & Raveesha, K. A. (2008). Antibacterial evaluation of some plant extracts against some human pathogenic bacteria. *Advances in Biological Research*, 2(3-4), 49-55.

Ncube, N. S., Afolayan, A. J., & Okoh, A. I. (2008). Assessment techniques of antimicrobial properties of natural compounds of plant origin: current methods and future trends. African Journal of Biotechnology, 7(12), 1797-1806.

Sherlock, O., Dolan, A., Athman, R., Power, A., Gethin, G., Cowman, S., & Humphreys, H. (2010). Comparison of the antimicrobial activity of Ulmo honey from Chile and Manuka honey against methicillin-resistant *Staphylococcus aureus*, *Escherichia coli* and *Pseudomonas aeruginosa*. *BMC Complementary and Alternative Medicine*, 10(1), 47.

Bose, P., Gupta, M., Kanti Mazumder, U., Sambath Kumar, R., Sivakumar, T., & Suresh Kumar, R. (2007). Hepatoprotective and antioxidant effects of Eupatorium ayapana against carbon tetrachloride induced hepatotoxicity in rats. *Iranian Journal of Pharmacology and Therapeutics*, 6(1), 27-33.

Raman N. Phytochemical Technique. New Indian Publishing Agencies: New Delhi, 2006. 19.

Rates, S. M. K. (2001). Plants as source of drugs. *Toxicon*, 39(5), 603-613.

Bisht, R., Katiyar, A., Singh, R., & Mittal, P. (2009). Antibiotic resistance-A global issue of concern. *Asian Journal of Pharmaceutical and Clinical Research*, 2(2), 34-39.

Roller, S. (1995). The quest for natural antimicrobials as novel means of food preservation: status report on a European research project. *International Biodeterioration & Biodegradation*, 36(3-4), 333-345.

Sewell, R. D. E., & Spencer, P. S. J. (1976). Antinociceptive activity of narcotic agonist and partial agonist analgesics and other agents in the tail-immersion test in mice and rats. *Neuropharmacology*, 15(11), 683-688.

Saravanan, P., Ramya, V., Sridhar, H., Balamurugan, V., & Umamaheswari, S. (2010). Antibacterial activity of *Allium sativum* L. on pathogenic bacterial strains. *Global Veterinaria*, 4(5), 519-522.

Oommen, S., Ved, D. K., & Krishnan, R. (2000). Tropical Indian medicinal plants: propagation methods. FRLHT, Foundation for Revitalisation of Local Health Traditions., 268-269.

Trivedi, M. N., Khemani, A., Vachhani, U. D., Shah, C. P., & Santani, D. D. (2011). Pharmacognostic, phytochemical analysis and antimicrobial activity of two Piper species. Pharmacie Globale, 7(05), 1-4.

Udgire, M. S., & Pathade, G. R. (2014). Bioassay directed fractionation and identification of bioactive components from root extract from *Piper longum*. International Journal of Bioassays, 3(5), 3016-3021.

Vane JR and Rotting BM. Overview, the mechanism of action of anti-inflammatory drugs. In Vane JR and Rotting BM. Clinical significance and potential of selective COX-2 inhibitors. London: William Harvey Press. 1998; 1-18.

Verpoorte, R., & Dihal, P. P. (1987). Medicinal plants of Surinam IV. Antimicrobial activity of some medicinal plants. *Journal of Ethnopharmacology*, 21(3), 315-318.

Winter, C. A., Risley, E. A., & Nuss, G. W. (1962). Carrageenin-induced edema in hind paw of the rat as an assay for anti-inflammatory drugs. Proceedings of the Society for Experimental Biology and Medicine, 111(3), 544-547.

Appendix

MEDIA COMPOSITION

Nutrient agar

Peptone	: 0.5g
Sodium chloride	: 0.8g
Beef extract	: 0.15g
Yeast extract	: 0.15g
Agar	: 1.5g
Distilled water	: 100ml
pH	: 7.4 ± 0.2

Mac conkey agar

Peptic digest of animal tissue	: 20g
Lactose	: 10g
Sodium tourocholate	: 5g
Neutral red	: 0.04g
Agar	: 20g
Distilled water	: 1000ml

MR-VP medium

Glucose phosphate medium

Peptone	: 0.25g
K_2HPO_4	: 0.5g
Glucose	: 0.25g
Distilled water	: 100ml
pH	: 6.9 ± 0.2

Muller Hinton agar

Beef extract	: 30g
Casein hydrolysate	: 17.5g
Starch	: 1.5g
Distilled water	: 100ml
Agar	: 15g
pH	: 7.5 ± 0.2

Sugars

Tripticase/peptone	: 1g
Carbohydrate	: 0.5g
Sodium chloride	: 1.5g
Phenol	: 0.001g

Indole

Tryptone	: 1g
NaCl	: 0.5g
Distilled water	: 100ml

Methyl red test

Glucose	: 0.5g
Peptone	: 0.5g
K_2HPO_4	: 0.5g
Distilled water	: 100ml
pH	: 6.9 ± 0.2

Voges-Proskauer reagent

Solution A	: 5% w/v solution
α-napthol	: 5g
Alcohol	: 100ml
Solution B	: 4% w/v solution
KOH	: 40g
Distilled water	: 100ml

Simmons citrate agar

Sodium citrate	: 0.2g
NaCl	: 0.5g
K_2HPO_4	: 0.1g
$NH_4H_2PO_4$	: 0.1g
$MgSO_4$	: 0.1g
Bromothymol blue	: 0.008g
Agar	: 1.5g
Distilled water	: 100ml
pH	: 6.8 ± 0.2

Triple sugar iron agar test

| Peptone | : 10g |

Yeast extract	: 3g
Beef extract	: 3g
Lactose	: 10g
Sucrose	: 10g
Dextrose	: 1g
Casein enzyme hydrolysate	: 10g
Sodium chloride	0.5g
Ferrous sulphate	: 0.2g
Sodium thiosulphate	: 0.3g
Phenol red	: 0.024g
Agar	: 12g
Distilled water	: 1000ml
pH	: 7.4 ± 0.2

Nitrate reduction test

Beef extract	: 0.3g
Peptone	: 0.5g
Potassium nitrate	: 0.1g
Distilled water	: 100ml
Agar	: 0.2g

Christensen's urea agar

Peptone	: 1g
Dextrose	: 1g
NaCl	: 5g
Monopotassium phosphate	: 2g
Agar	: 0.12g
Phenol red	: 15g
Distilled water	: 1000ml
pH	: 6.8 ± 0.2

Mannitol motility

Peptone	: 1g
NaCl	: 0.75g
Beef extract	: 0.1g
Mannitol	: 1g

Agar	: 1.5g
Phenol red	: 0.0025g
Distilled water	: 100ml
pH	: 6.8 ± 0.2

Kovac's reagent

Butanol	: 75ml
p-dimethylaminobenzaldehyde	: 5g
Concentrated HCl	: 25ml
pH	: 6.3 ± 0.2